How to Speak "Horse"

A Horse-Crazy Kid's Guide to Reading Body Language and "Talking Back"

Andrea & Markus Eschbach

Photos by Horst Stretferdt
Translated by Julia Welling

TRAFALGAR SQUARE
North Pomfret, Vermont

First published in 2012 by
Trafalgar Square Books
North Pomfret, Vermont 05053

Printed in China

Originally published in the German language as *Pferdesprache für Kinder* by
Franckh-Kosmos Verlags-GmbH & Co. KG, Stuttgart

Disclaimer of Liability
The author and publisher shall have neither liability nor responsibility to any person or entity with
respect to any loss or damage caused or alleged to be caused directly or indirectly by the information
contained in this book. While the book is as accurate as the author can make it, there may be errors,
omissions, and inaccuracies.

Trafalgar Square Books encourages the use of approved safety helmets in all equestrian
sports and activities.

ISBN: 978-1-57076-532-2

Library of Congress Control Number: 2012941879

All photos by Horst Streitferdt, Stuttgart, except: p. 13 (top) by Juniors
Bildarchiv, Ruhpolding, and p. 1 by Christiane Slawik, Würzburg

Cover design by RM Didier
Typefaces: Charter ITC by BT, Matrix Script

10 9 8 7 6 5 4 3 2

Contents

Hi!

Our names are Andrea and Markus, and we are horse trainers. Since we are horse lovers, we decided to turn our hobby into our profession.

If *you* are as passionate about horses as *we* are, join us in this book as we take you on a journey into the fascinating world of the horse. We will show you how you can learn to understand the language of horses and—even better—how they can learn to understand *you*.

"Talking" or "whispering" to horses can sometimes sound a little farfetched to the inexperienced person, but with our help and guidance you will soon learn that this is very much a legitimate and effective practice. You will learn to communicate with your horse as if he is your best friend!

We hope you have fun reading this book and wish you an exciting journey!

Yours,

Andrea and Markus

The Secret of How to Speak "Horse"

"Horse whispering" does not mean that we actually whisper something in our horse's ear—a magic word, for example, that makes him do everything we want. Horse whisperers are people who use near invisible signals to communicate with (or "speak to") their horses. In tune to these signals, the horse does as commanded—there is no need for pulling or yanking on the reins, and no spurs or whips are involved. And best of all: ***Everyone*** can learn how to speak horse!

Horse Language

Instead of words, horses use subtle, almost invisible signals to "talk" to each other. They move their whole body, or just parts of it, such as their ears or tail. Horses seldom talk through audible sounds but instead rely mostly on body language. If you learn what these subtle signals in the horse's body mean, you will be able to use them to talk to your horse. A horse whisperer applies these body language signals whenever he is around horses.

Your horse will learn to follow you if you know how to speak "horse" to him.

Communication is what this book is about: It is worth learning the horse's language so he can quickly understand what you want to tell him and what you want from him! As you will see, it is not difficult to make your horse understand you. With our help, the two of you will soon "talk" to each other about everything!

Have you ever wondered how a herd of horses determines its leader? A horse will approach the leader of the herd without attracting much attention. If the lead horse is a good and attentive one, she (the leader is usually a mare) will quickly acknowledge the approach and send the signals back to ensure the other horse keeps a respectful distance. Horses test us in the same playful manner. As long as we continue to earn and deserve their respect, they will happily be our partners in life. It gives them peace of mind to know and understand their boundaries.

What Do Horses Do All Day?

The best way to learn to speak the horse's language is by observing them. What do they do when they are together in the pasture? Who grazes? Who plays? How do horses invite each other to play? What does an ordinary day in the life of a horse look like?

Horses are **herbivores**: They are constant grazers, and in the wild, they eat grass, herbs, and leaves. They love to roam open plains.

With their long legs, horses are exceptional **runners**. When they get scared, they will run away. This is why they are known as **animals of flight**. In the wild, a hungry lion would leave empty-handed when the horse has time to run.

Horses put a great deal of value in their companions. A group of horses is called a **herd**, and in it, horses feel safe and secure.

These horses are grazing. Their relaxed body language shows that they feel secure in their environment.

Through mutual grooming horses deepen friendships and build a strong sense of community in the herd.

Foals really enjoy playing and testing each other's speed and strength.

"Do not disturb me, I am taking a break!" Horses often doze in a standing position, which is comfortable for them and enables them to quickly react to signs of danger. But foals like this one often choose to lie down to sleep, even in the middle of the pasture—they know their mother is keeping an eye on them!

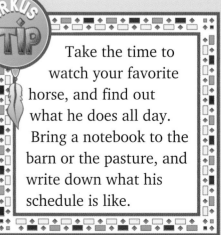

MARKUS TIP

Take the time to watch your favorite horse, and find out what he does all day. Bring a notebook to the barn or the pasture, and write down what his schedule is like.

Playing by the Rules
—Living in a Herd

A herd consists of many individuals who live and work together and form a unit. In order for a large group to function harmoniously, every individual needs to know exactly what his or her task is. Horses have a system, a **hierarchy**, in which every horse has his place.

The leader of a horse herd is usually a mare. In the same way you watch out for your friends, the lead mare looks out for her herd. The individuals of the herd are connected to each other in their thoughts and feelings, and in this way can sense when something is wrong. The herd looks to its lead mare to lead its members to safe pasture grounds, watering holes, and rest areas. The lead mare has to make sure that all members of the herd stick together and that the herd as a unit is cared for.

The lead mare is the boss: She demands obedience and respect from the other horses. She has the right to eat first and to drink first when the herd reaches a source of water. Lead mares are smart, caring, and dominant. Every horse knows exactly where he or she is positioned in the herd hierarchy.

You can tell horses' ranks by the way in which they keep a certain distance and stand at a certain angle to each other.

Keeping Order in the Herd

The highest ranking individual—the lead mare or alpha animal—has the most authority, and also the most responsibility in the task of securing the survival of the entire herd. That means a lot of work and requires a lot of experience! The lower ranking individuals also have an important task: They have to immediately follow the orders of the alpha animal without asking questions. They will only do this if they are absolutely sure that the lead mare knows how to take care of them and that they can trust her. Therefore, the herd must also challenge the lead mare all the time. The members of the herd always need to know how good their boss really is.

Challenging Means Quality Control

When you are around horses you will notice that they will test you in the same manner! What they are trying to find out is if they can trust that you are in control so they can feel comfortable and safe when you are around—just like when they challenge a lead mare in a herd.

Danger!

When horses are in danger—say a predator is approaching, for example—their *instinct* (inner drive) is to run away immediately. In order to get to safety as quickly as possible, horses flee in an orderly fashion: one after the other, the highest ranking animal leads the group and the lowest ranking individual follows last. It is much easier to flee in an organized manner than in a wild panic! Even though the horses we own and ride do not have to run away from lions and cougars, they still have the instinct to flee from danger. Nature provided them with this behavior in order for them to have the best chance of surviving over time.

ANDREA TIP

Make a list of all the traits that you value in your best friend. Why is he or she your best friend? What makes *you* a good friend to others? It is important to recognize these characteristics when talking to horses.

The Horse's Senses

Horses are very sensitive beings. Their senses are much more acute than ours. Through sight, hearing, smell, taste, and touch, horses explore their surroundings at an earlier age, more quickly, and in more detail than us. In the wild, they have to quickly detect potential danger because other animals see them as prey. Their acute senses help them do that.

Ears

Horses' ears stick out noticeably and are very flexible. Because of this, horses are able to listen to sounds all around them and to hear when a predator is approaching the herd. The ears also tell others how the horse is feeling (his mood).

Eyes

With their large and slightly protruding eyes, horses are able to get a good overview of their surroundings. Their eyes are positioned on the sides of their head, which increases their field of vision. A large field of vision means that horses can see what is happening both next to and behind them, even without turning their head— they can see far more of what is going on around them than we can see around us! This way, horses can detect an approaching predator early on and flee quickly.

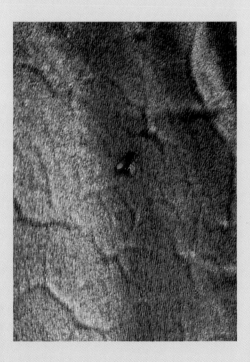

Skin and Coat

Horses are so sensitive to touch, they can feel a fly landing on their coat.

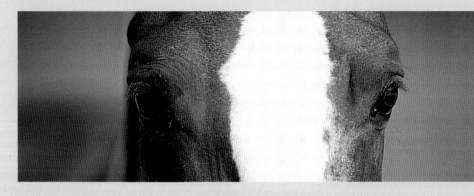

Nostrils and Whiskers

The horse's sense of smell is well-developed: In order to better identify a smell, the horse can flare his nostrils. Horses who don't know each other will sniff at one another to find out if they get along ("You smell friendly!") Horses also have whiskers on their face that actually improve their sense of touch. When they graze, it is easy for them to feel what the surrounding ground is like.

wWhen grazing and eating in general, horses need to know the difference between what is edible and what is not. If you watch your horse eat, you will see that he has no difficulty differentiating between small stones and kernels of grain, for example, without even looking at his feed. In addition, the horse's tongue helps him detect the taste of sweet grasses and aromatic herbs he needs in his diet.

When horses smell particularly strong scents, they often show the *flehmen response*—they curl their upper lip up and out. This looks a little as if they are laughing.

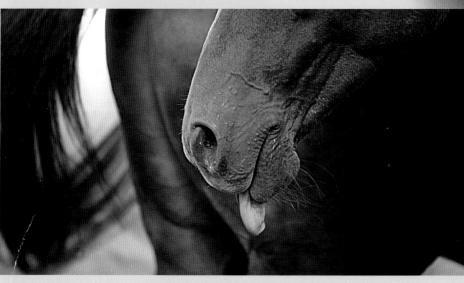

The Language of Horses

In order to understand the language of horses you have to observe them closely: How do horses communicate and what do they use to do so? Which "words" do horses use? What do specific "words" mean? One thing you will quickly discover: Horses use body language! We have developed a mini "language course" in horse-speak to help you learn how to talk to your horse. Begin by learning to understand and use the "horse words and phrases" on these pages!

Horse-Speak Dictionary

"Oh, yum! You brought something good to eat!"

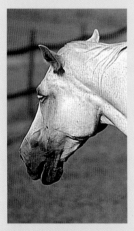

"I'm yawning."

"I'm resting."

"I'm tired."

"I don't feel like doing this."

"May I come closer?"

"I want to get out of here!"

"Hi! Who are you?"

"I like you."

"I don't like you. Go away! Don't come closer—I'm warning you!"

"Please, keep scratching!"

"One step closer and I will bite you."

Horses show you what they are feeling through body language. Horses can also attract attention by using their voice: They can whinny loudly to call out for or greet their friends. When they whinny quietly, they are happy about something. When horses relax, they exhale a deep and quick breath through their nostrils, just like when you *sigh*. If the horse is excited or tense or dust has gotten in his nose, he will repeatedly snort loudly and blow out air through his nostrils.

MARKUS TIP

We can use our hands, arms, legs, feet, breathing, voice, and facial expressions in order to communicate with each other and with animals. Almost all forms of communication, whether between humans or humans and animals, happens without words.

"I don't like this at all!"

"Being free is awesome!"

Horses and Humans

Horses are big and very strong animals. In comparison to them, humans are small and weak. When push comes to shove, there is no bridle or lead rope, no stick or chain with which we are able to control such an energetic and powerful animal. It is impossible to make horses do what you want by using force. As you have learned, the horse is a flight animal, and this means he will quickly feel trapped and threatened. He will always react in a manner most consistent with his nature, and when flight is impossible because the horse is tied, for example, then he will panic and react violently. He might kick, bite, rear, or buck. This behavior is very dangerous for us, the small, weak humans that we are!

How Your Horse Sees You

To horses, humans belong in the "predator" category. Why? Because we look like one. If you think about it, you will find many similarities between the human body and those of cougars or grizzlies, for example.

Our eyes are located in the front of our head.

Our ears are rather small and do not stick out.

Our hands and fingers look like claws.

We often lead our horse in a manner that reminds him of a predator: The lead rope is held very short and one of our hands holds it right below the horse's chin. It is better to keep some distance between you and your horse when you lead him. Use a long lead rope that you can hold loosely in your hands. When we bridle our horse we also behave like predators (while wondering why our four-legged friend is protesting!) We reach for the nose of the horse and grab for his highly sensitive head, which we then hold tightly so it will not get away. To the horse, this is additional evidence that we must be predators!

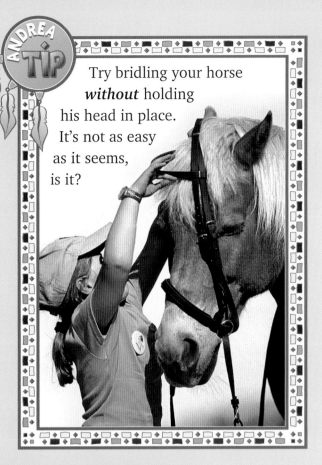

ANDREA TIP

Try bridling your horse *without* holding his head in place. It's not as easy as it seems, is it?

When we are around horses, the first thing we have to do is make the horse understand that we are *not* dangerous and that they do not need to be afraid of us. We can do this by *not* behaving like a predator. Unfortunately, we cannot change our body in a way that makes us look more like a horse and less like a grizzly bear, but we can *learn* to move and behave more like a horse!

Make Your Horse Your Friend

You can learn to get your horse to do what you want in a way that is positive and kind. Using "horse speak" makes it easier for him to understand your commands and ensures he will not be afraid of you. In this way, your horse will learn to trust you and will become your friend.

The idea behind "horse whispering" is that you use the signals and language naturally found in horses in order to tell your own horse what you wish him to do. You behave in patterns familiar to the horse—postures and movements he might have learned as a young horse in a herd or that he may have been born with. You behave just like another horse would, and more specifically, like a **lead horse** would: confident and determined yet friendly.

This Is What You Need

Even though you can talk to horses basically everywhere, it is easier to do at first in a confined area. We like to use a round pen, which is a small, round arena encircled by a sturdy fence. You can also temporarily "fence off" a small area within a regular riding arena. Your horse can wear a halter, but he does not have to—and we feel your "conversation" can be more natural without one. Hold a 10-foot lead rope to help steer your horse or to keep him at a distance if need be. The goal is for your horse to move freely within the confined area while you use subtle movements of your body to ask him to stop, slow down, speed up, or turn. You are working on learning to control your horse's movements from a distance and without touching him.

The "leader's" position (*your* position) is in the middle of the training area. We call it the "office." The horse is only allowed to enter your office when you ask him to. Otherwise, he should move around the track just inside the fence line. When you and your horse are in the round pen together, you should know where he is and what he is doing at all times.

When you are ready to ask your horse to do something, look right at him and **concentrat**e.

By aiming your focus and arm gesture at the hindquarters, you can ask your horse to go forward.

By aiming your focus and arm gesture at the shoulder, you can ask your horse to turn.

By aiming your focus and arm gesture at the head, you can ask your horse to slow down or stop.

MARKUS TIP

When you first learn to "speak horse" in the arena or round pen, you should do so with a knowledgeable trainer or instructor present. A good trainer will guide you as you learn to use your horse's language. And remember, if at any time you start to feel uncomfortable working with your horse, do not hesitate to tell your trainer! Do not try to do an exercise if you are afraid or do not understand. Ask your trainer for help!

In order to make your horse move the way you want, you have to learn to use the right amount of strength and energy in your posture and focus. Even though you are not touching the horse, this is called **pressure** because the sensitive horse can "feel" your body language. In the beginning, apply as little pressure as possible and increase the amount until your horse reacts as you would like. Then immediately **stop** facing him and **stop** focusing on your specific instruction. When you **stop** it is called the **release**.

Think, breathe in, and focus your eyes.

Click your tongue and point with your hand.

Swing or toss the rope as an extension of your arm.

Your goal is to create a connection with your horse and make the way you communicate through that connection more and more subtle. Eventually, it will feel like you lead your horse by an invisible thread—completely without force.

15

Speaking "Horse" — Let's Get Started

Horses like to live where there is lots of space—on open plains or in large pastures, for example. The more members a herd has, the more space it needs. Horses use little games to establish the rules for their community depending on the area they live in: who has to stand where, who is allowed to come close to the lead mare and at what angle, who can eat first, and so on. Every interaction has meaning and serves to establish a horse's place in the hierarchy of the herd.

Defining Spaces

Begin to learn how to define space with your horse while you are playing with your horse and talking to him in the arena or round pen. As you move around the area **without** asking him to do anything, watch his reactions from the corner of your eye. Does he spook, run away, stop, turn his back toward you, or come toward you? Any reaction to your movement and position is fine—it is up to your horse to decide what to do. In this exercise, you are not holding him or giving him a task. You are simply establishing contact and ideas of space.

By stepping confidently in an area to the rear of the horse (a safe distance away) you show the horse that you would like the space to yourself and that you are the leader or alpha animal.

"This is my personal space. Whoever enters without asking is showing a lack of respect!"

"I decide how close you may come to me!"

Driving Forward

The first thing you want to ask your horse to do is **move forward**. Horses have a natural urge to move and run so this direction should be really easy for the horse and a positive place for you to start. The exercise is important even though it might seem easy. **Who drives others forward** and **who moves when driven** is an important issue within the herd that defines which horse is higher ranking. If you are able to send your horse forward, he will take this as proof that you are his boss and accept you as such. In a way, you are playing a game and each time you move your horse forward, you get points. The one who has the most points is the boss! To drive your horse forward, imagine you want

Position yourself slightly behind and to the side of your horse to send him forward: Your horse will see that the area in front of him is open and move in that direction.

to"push" him forward with your eyes: Stare at your horse's hindquarters as if your eyes can do the pushing. Your horse will be able to feel the energy you send out and will move away from it.

If necessary, you can intensify your signals to move forward with a swing of the rope.

You can ask your horse to move forward even faster by tossing the end of the rope in the direction of his hindquarters.

Ask one of your friends to approach you slowly while you decide how close he or she may come. Pay attention to when you feel comfortable and when you start to feel crowded. Mark the spot on the ground so you can see how much space you need to yourself and how close other people can come before you grow uncomfortable. Is this space different when you are around people you do not know well?

When you need lots of energy to get him moving, you can swing the rope around in your hand like a propeller.

17

Controlling Speed and Stopping

You want to have control over your horse no matter how fast he is going. Practice talking to him at all gaits. Your horse should accelerate in a relaxed and easy manner, move at a constant speed, change gaits, and stop whenever you ask him to.

*Whether at a walk, trot or canter—if **you** are able to control your horse's gait and speed, you will feel confident and enjoy how fun it can be working together with your four-legged friend.*

Stopping

You already learned that horses have the innate urge to run forward. They usually have no problem accelerating. So *before* you ask your horse to move *faster*, make sure to check his brakes! If you are able to stop your horse from a distance without any problems, you already have good basic control over his legs. If you discover, however, that you have a hard time making your horse stop, even though all your signals to stop are correct, you really need to practice "braking" before moving on. Not only is this important in groundwork, but it might be that your horse is also difficult to stop or to control when you ride him—and that can be very dangerous.

MARKUS TIP

Make sure you remain in the center of the round pen or arena (in your "office") when you are asking your horse to slow down or stop. If you move toward the fence, you will get too close to your horse and he might run into you by accident.

When you want your horse to slow down or stop, stand at a considerable distance in front and slightly to the side of your horse and "block" the open path ahead of him. Every time you breathe out, relax your body. Horses are so sensitive that they can see and feel the change in your posture. They will relax and slow down as a consequence. You can increase the effect of the "brakes" if needed by making big arm movements like dropping a stop flag in front of the horse.

If your horse does not come to a halt when you use subtle signals, toss the rope at his front end in an assertive manner in order to gain his attention.

19

"Release" and Change of Direction

In horse language, the best way to tell your horse, "Good job!" and "Yes!" is as follows: At exactly the same moment your horse has followed your command correctly, direct all your energy and attention *away* from him. As we discussed earlier, this is called the *release* because you are "turning off" the pressure of your body language and focus. For your horse, this means he has the time and space to take a deep breath.

For a short moment, give your horse a release by turning your back toward him or maybe taking a step away from him. He will soon realize that it pays off to comply with your requests. Every time he does, he is rewarded with a short break. These breaks are also very important because your horse uses them to "digest" what he has just learned.

When you need to say, "No, that is not what I wanted," your attention, your eyes, and your body remain focused on the horse—that is, the pressure persists. If your horse resists, increase the energy you are sending his way and intensify your commands. The second you recognize even the slightest attempt by your horse to accept your signals, reduce the intensity of your posture and focus to say, "Yes."

Change of Direction

Once you are able to control your horse's speed through subtle signals, it is time that you also learn how to steer him more quietly and efficiently. Remember, *you* decide in which direction your horse's legs are supposed to move and when. In order to ask for a change of direction, you must be able to change your horse's speed, as well. If you cannot control the "horsepower," you will have less influence on the steering wheel!

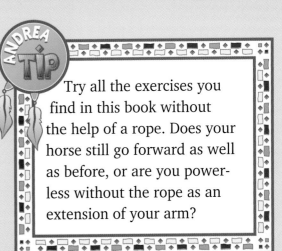

ANDREA TIP

Try all the exercises you find in this book without the help of a rope. Does your horse still go forward as well as before, or are you powerless without the rope as an extension of your arm?

Turn to the Outside

*To ask your horse to turn to the outside, begin by holding the rope in the hand that is at the head of the horse—so if your horse is **going left** around the round pen or arena, the rope is in your **left hand**. You do this so you are ready to drive your horse forward once he has turned in the other direction. Stand to the front and side of your horse, in the center of the round pen, and give him a moment to pause and think about what to do next.*

To make your horse turn, move your arms as if you want to push against your horse's inside cheek so his head goes toward the fence. You want his legs to keep moving during the entire turn, so continue to encourage forward movement.

As your horse turns toward the outside, move behind him and focus on his hindquarters to keep him moving in the new direction without hesitating.

Turn to the Inside

Begin with the rope in the hand at the front of your horse, as when you ask him to turn to the outside. Move parallel to your horse at a swift pace. Then accelerate until you are walking ahead of your horse and he can see your back. As soon as he takes a step toward the inside of the circle, turn around to face him.

Point the hand with the rope at the horse's outside cheek (the one that was closest to the fence) to tell him that you want him to continue stepping to the inside and then return to the fence facing the opposite direction.

Focus energy toward your horse's hindquarters to encourage him to move forward in the new direction. Note that turning to the outside is more of a direction, and turning to the inside is an invitation.

Follow Me!

When your horse has decided that he likes to change direction by turning to the inside when you invite him to, you can ask him to come to you to the center of the round pen or arena. A good leader decides when the horse is allowed to approach. Ask your horse to come to you in a confident manner, and immediately stroke him on the neck and praise him to strengthen the friendship between the two of you.

In order to invite your horse to follow you, turn your back toward him and take a small step forward. Then stop and see what happens.

When your horse sees your back turned toward him, he knows that in "horse speak" this means, "Follow me!" He will decide if he wants to approach you or not.

When the horse chooses to come to you at your invitation, he has accepted you as his leader.

What to Do If ...

This is too close!

...your horse is supposed to stay to the outside along the fence, but he comes inside toward you: Stare at his shoulder, and point your hand at it, too, to make him return to the outside track.

...you leave your "office" in the center of the ring and before you know it, you have moved really close to your horse: This tends to happen when you are trying really hard to make your horse do something. A mark on the ground in the center of the round pen can help you maintain a safe distance.

... your horse decides to run away from a certain exercise: This is often the case when you ask your horse to do something he does not like or when something scares him. Remember, horses are flight animals. When your horse tries to "get away" from a request by moving faster, turn him to the outside. But, make sure you keep a safe distance between the two of you!

...your horse wants to turn to the inside, toward you, instead of to the outside, like you want him to: The second you realize that your horse is going to try to turn to the inside, make him stop and come to a halt. If your horse has already made a full turn to the inside, ask him to return to the outside track as quickly as possible and then ask him to move forward in the same direction as before.

A Few Notes to Keep You Safe

It is usually loads of fun doing groundwork with your horse loose in the round pen or arena as described here. However, horses tend to easily get scared and can start running in the blink of an eye. Keep an eye on your horse at all times, even when you have turned away to give him a break or to invite him to come to you. You can take a peek at him by looking over your shoulder without staring at him directly. Whenever possible, ask your trainer or instructor to help you. He or she might be able to prevent dangerous situations from developing and can help you when you run into problems. When an exercise does not turn out as you planned, try to get it right **no more than** five times. If you make more unsuccessful attempts, you will weaken your position as leader.

MARKUS TIP

Place a plastic drink bottle on a table or post and toss your rope at it. If you can knock it down, you have good focus and control.

Everyday
Horse Language

When you can complete the exercises in this book you will notice that the two of you can understand each other more easily and quickly. Your horse will pay more attention to what you are asking anytime you are together, and his reactions will become more precise.

For example, all of a sudden, it will become much easier for you to catch your horse in the pasture. You simply have to look at him with focus, then turn away and invite him to follow you—it will not take long for him to come toward you as soon as you enter the pasture. When grooming him, all you will have to do to get him to step aside is press your hand against his hindquarters. He will obediently move over and make room for you to brush him. Everything is going

to be easier and more effortless—without all the little power struggles most people assume come as part of handling horses. Your horse will feel more comfortable with you because he understands you better and is able to react more quickly to your requests, and he feels assured that *you* understand *him* better, too.

You will realize how much fun it is to play with and train your horse as the invisible connection of your partnership becomes stronger and stronger! Once you have discovered this feeling, you will never get enough of it!

More Safety Tips

- Do not approach your horse directly from behind. He might be startled and kick out. Approach him from the front and side so he can see you. You can also use your voice to announce your presence.

- Do not allow your horse to approach you without being invited. If he comes too close, he might step on your toes, shove you, or in some cases maybe nip or bite you.

- If you want to give your horse a treat, give it to him *after* your training session but *before* you take him back to his pasture friends. Never enter a pasture or paddock with treats when there is more than one horse in it.

- If your horse gets spooked and excited, breathe out, talk to him in a calm and friendly voice, pat him, and move around in a calm and relaxed manner until he is no longer tense. He will feel your calmness, which inspires trust that you will keep him safe as his leader.

- Know that some horses may have never learned to respect human beings. These horse can be really dangerous, and they belong only in the hands of an experienced horse trainer.

ANDREA TIP

What do your parents or teachers say or do when you do well at home or at school? What does a mare say to her foal? These are important lessons in how you and your horse can come to understand each other.

Things That Are Important to Us

Always keep in mind that horses are living beings with feelings and needs. Nature has created them in a way so that their actions and behavior serve their survival. This means that a horse's every action has a reason and a meaning. Our challenge as the humans who love them is to find out why they do what they do.

Horses are very different from us. They often feel threatened by things that, from our perspective, are harmless, and they may react in ways that are completely irrational to us. The problem is, we use our *human eye*s to understand the behavior of horses. Once we learn to see our surroundings with the *eyes of a horse*, we create the basis for true horsemanship.

Violence is never an option to make a horse compliant. When he feels fear, pain, or stress, he cannot learn. Calmness, determination, and kindness will get your horse to cooperate much more quickly. He will not only learn new things, he will learn to enjoy doing them.

Every day, you have the chance to discover new things in the world of horses. When we are willing to accept horses as the amazing and unbelievably patient teachers they are, we can allow them to help us understand them better. In this way, they become our friends.

Goodbye!

We hope that you enjoyed our little course in "horse speak"! Now you have the necessary tools to become a true horse whisperer! Before we go, we want to share a little secret with you: The better you are able to handle your horse from the ground, the better he will be under saddle! The groundwork exercises you do in the round pen will help you and your horse with your riding performance, in and out of the ring. We hope you keep having tons of fun with the most beautiful animals in the world: horses!

Yours,

Andrea and Markus

We want to thank everyone who assisted us with the pictures in this book, as well as San Jon, the farm in Graubünden, Switzerland, where the photographs were taken.

Andrea & Markus Eschbach

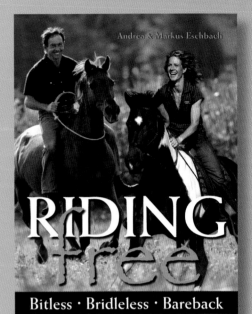